AT HOME WITH
Quilts

NANCY J. MARTIN

That Patchwork Place®

Mission Statement

WE ARE DEDICATED TO PROVIDING
QUALITY PRODUCTS AND SERVICES
THAT INSPIRE CREATIVITY.
WE WORK TOGETHER TO ENRICH
THE LIVES WE TOUCH.

That Patchwork Place is a
financially responsible
ESOP company.

Credits

Photography Brent Kane
(except where noted)
Editorial Director Kerry I. Hoffman
Technical Editors Ursula Reikes
Sharon Rose
Barbara Weiland
Managing Editor Greg Sharp
Copy Editor Liz McGehee
Proofreader Melissa Riesland
Design Director Judy Petry
Designer Kay Green
Production Assistant Shean Bemis

At Home with Quilts
©1996 by Nancy J. Martin

That Patchwork Place, Inc.
PO Box 118
Bothell, WA 98041-0118
USA

Printed in Hong Kong
01 00 99 98 97 96   6 5 4 3 2 1

Cover photo: The living room of Diana and
Chris Schmidt (see pages 54–59) features
two Postage Stamp quilts (on the chairs)
and a variety of collectibles.

*Photos and text in this book were originally
published in* Make Room for Quilts, *©1994.*

Martin, Nancy J.
At home with quilts / Nancy J. Martin.
p. cm.
ISBN 1-56477-157-1
1. Quilts in interior decoration. I. Title.
NK2115.5.Q54M37 1996
746.46–dc20   96-33763
CIP

Acknowledgments

To the homeowners who graciously allowed us to photograph their lovely homes;

To Brent Kane, whose sense of adventure was captured by this new experience of photographing room settings;

To Cleo Nollette, who helped sew to meet decorating deadlines for the photo sessions;

To Anita Yesland, who kept the remodel on schedule; and to Barry Wilcox, Steve Worley, Andy Fredrickson, and Greg Ballard, who did the carpentry;

To Cherry Jarvis, who encouraged me and provided a quiet place to write;

And especially to Dan Martin, who endured yet another remodeling project.

Contents

Introduction

Quilts and quiltmaking have been part of my life for more than twenty years. I've pieced more than two hundred quilt tops, collected and enjoyed a sizable number of antique quilts, cuddled under quilts on cold winter nights, and used quilts in the decor of every room in my house. Quilts warm more than the body; they soothe the soul while bringing a splash of color to an otherwise ho-hum room.

Family quilts bring fond memories and recollections of the aunt, mother, or grandmother who made them. The quilts connect us to their lives and bring us a special comfort. Often humble in origin, perhaps made of snippets of fabric found in the scrap bag, these quilts have texture and color that add a softness to our busy lives. A scrap of one of our school dresses or shirts, or a favorite apron of our mother's found amidst the patches reminds us to slow down and enjoy the simple pleasures from times past, because life passes all too quickly.

Collecting quilts can add a new dimension to our lives. We feel especially connected to history when we look at the wonderful fabrics in old quilts. Happily, we can care for and store antique quilts using good conservation techniques, and still allow them to contribute to the decor of a room.

Jonathan Holstein and Gail Van der Hoof noted the graphic appeal of quilts when they organized the first major museum exhibition of quilts at New York's Whitney Museum of American Art in 1971. The exhibit led Jonathan Holstein to write a book, *The Pieced Quilt–An American Design Tradition*. He wrote:

> It would be encouraging to think that American women would thus continue the tradition begun by their sisters over three centuries ago. . . . The best of their designs, based on those fundamental geometric forms which are agelessly

Fred Milkie, Jr.

4

beautiful, have that vitality, freshness, and validity which are the moving qualities of distinguished visual objects of any type, and of any place or time.

There is no doubt quilts have a nostalgic appeal that ties us to simpler times, free of modern technology. As John Naisbitt explains in his book *Megatrends*:

The need for compensatory high touch is everywhere. The more high tech in our society, the more we will want to create high-touch environments, with soft edges balancing the hard edges of technology.

As we moved through the 1970s, industrialization and its technology moved more and more from the workplace to the home. High-tech furniture echoed the glories of an industrial past.... But the brief period of interest in high-tech furniture and minimalist design was just that—brief. It is now behind us. Ahead of us for a long period is the emphasis on high touch and comfort to counterbalance a world going mad with high technology.

Among other things, this means soft colors—pastels are becoming quite popular—coziness, plumpness, the unconstructed look, and links to the past. Folk art is the perfect counterpoint to a computerized society. No wonder handmade quilts are so popular.

As men and women endeavor to create home environments that bring comfort and tranquillity, a quilt, whether spread on a bed or hung on a wall, is probably the one single element that can quickly achieve that goal.

If you are not lucky enough to have inherited family quilts, and your budget doesn't allow for collecting quilts, you might consider making a quilt or wall hanging for your home. The process is relatively easy and doesn't require any special skills, just a willingness to read and carefully follow directions. It's rather like assembling a jigsaw puzzle, and those who enjoy that experience will do well. It also gives artistic people the opportunity to work with color and pattern.

The joy of quiltmaking is in the process, working with the fabric to make a pleasing arrangement of pattern and texture. What is this magical textile known as the quilt? Technically, it consists of three layers (a quilt top, batting sandwiched in the middle, and backing) held together with either hand or machine stitching. More than that, a quilt is a work of art that brings color and comfort into our lives. As it hangs on a wall, it softens the environment, absorbing noise. As it covers our bodies, it brings warmth, comfort, and a flood of memories that lull us into serenity.

Scrappy quilts combined with chintz pillows and Battenberg lace accents highlight the striped denim sofas and draw the eye to a dramatic view.

Decorating with Quilts

WHERE DO I BEGIN?

Decorating with quilts involves more than hanging one on the wall or tossing another over the back of a rocker. A quilt, like a modern painting, is a bold graphic element that can serve as a focal point for an entire room or as part of a grouping that accessorizes a room.

If you want a special quilt to be the room's focus, it should be the starting point for your decorating scheme. If it will be an accessory, consider the color scheme, style, and theme of the room before selecting and placing the quilt. The quilt's size, color, and theme dictates its use within a room.

CREATE A CENTER OF INTEREST

A fireplace, a bay window, a window wall that overlooks a stunning view, a stone wall, or a staircase are all examples of architectural details around which a room can be styled. If your room has a strong feature, make it the focal point and hang a quilt on the opposite wall. The quilt becomes a secondary area of interest.

Many of today's homes lack such architectural elements. This makes design decisions and furniture arrangements more challenging. If your room lacks an architectural detail to serve as the decor's focal point, invent one: hang a quilt on the wall and allow it to dictate your furniture arrangement and color scheme.

A strong graphic quilt can serve as a focal point.

STYLE

Furniture type, color scheme, and accessories all contribute to the style of a room. Style can range from frilly, romantic Victorian, to rough-hewn rustic, to clean-lined contemporary. Fortunately for us, quiltmaking is a versatile art, incorporating an infinite variety of styles. It is possible to find the perfect quilt for almost any setting.

An antique quilt, striped pillows, and lace complement the floral chintz comforter.

Romantic

Soft pastel rooms full of floral prints, lace tablecloths, ruffled pillows, and delicate quilts create a romantic feeling. Floral prints abound in colors perfect for this decorating theme. Wicker furniture, dried flowers, and quilts all contribute to a relaxed and gracious environment.

Country

This is the style we most frequently associate with quilts. Early American furniture, braided or hooked rugs, plaid upholstery, and Country memorabilia are often used with scrappy-looking quilts or appliqué quilts done in the folk-art style. This creates a warm, comfortable setting, ideal for a relaxed lifestyle.

Scrap quilts, composed of many fabrics, are part of the Country look.

Rustic

The Adirondack or "lodge" look has emerged as a folksy decorating style, rugged in feeling. Natural textures, such as stone or exposed logs, together with wide-plank wood floors, form the foundation. Twig furniture, Indian blankets or rugs, fishing gear, and oxidized metal objects work naturally with wool quilts, flannel throws, or scrappy quilts made from homespun plaids and dramatic checks. You can add textural contrast and lighten the look with Battenberg lace or cutwork tablecloths and curtains.

Wool quilts or quilts with strong motifs work well with rustic twig furniture.

Traditional

A traditional setting contains more formal furniture and fabrics. Wall-to-wall carpeting is often layered with Oriental rugs. Upholstery fabrics are deeper in tone and incorporate lustrous weaves and fibers, such as brocades, jacquards, silks, and taffetas. The room's glow is reflected in brass lamps and polished wood. Deeply colored dramatic quilts, contemporary art quilts, or richly embellished Crazy quilts enhance classic furniture and create a sumptuous backdrop for entertaining.

Richly embellished Crazy quilts and contemporary art quilts blend with a traditional setting.

Contemporary

Contemporary rooms are often characterized by neutral color schemes, well-cushioned furniture, and wall-to-wall carpeting or highly polished hardwood floors. Beige, gray, and taupe often serve as background colors on walls and floors. Crisp, striped sofas and chairs, Parson's tables, and modern lighting all highlight contemporary wall hangings. This is an upscale style that can strikingly emphasize a single quilt.

The neutral color scheme of a contemporary room highlights the art quilt on the wall.

Eclectic

Eclectic rooms combine a variety of styles along with a few unusual touches. Rather than a collection of small accessories, one dramatic piece, such as a large painting, a weathervane, or even a birdhouse can be used to create a comfortable, yet dramatic, atmosphere—one that refuses to take itself too seriously.

The bright yellow fabric in the Bear's Paw quilt enlivens this eclectic room.

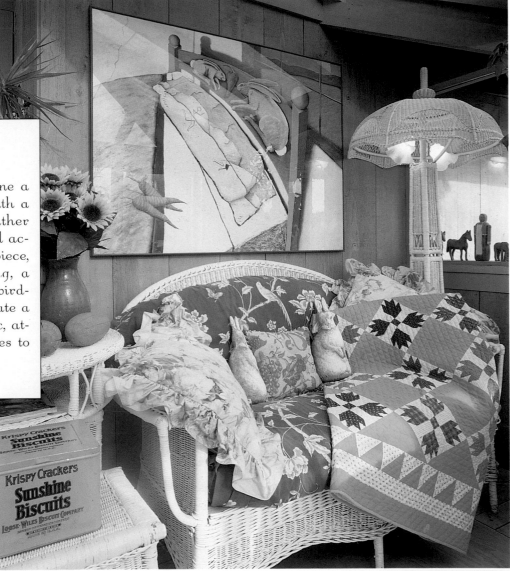

How Do I Choose Fabrics and Colors to Match My Quilts?

Choosing color for a room is often the most difficult decision. Yet color is the single most important element in room decor. It creates a mood or expresses an idea. Remember that background areas—walls, ceiling, and floor—represent almost two-thirds of the color in a room. Take this into account when looking at color swatches: use large swatches for dominant colors and small swatches for accent colors to see how they will interact.

<u>Use a neutral background.</u> Rooms with neutral backgrounds are tranquil and allow you to accent with texture and bolder colors. Match the color of the walls and ceilings and use light-colored wood or carpet on the floor. The room will appear larger, and your quilt will become the dominant element.

<u>Create warmth.</u> A warm color scheme is excellent for rooms that receive little natural light. Use red, orange, yellow, tan, or warm brown to create a cozy feeling. Remember that warm colors dominate and ap-

pear to come forward, making a room seem smaller.

<u>Cool a warm room.</u> To cool down a room, especially one with a sunny southern exposure, use colors such as green, blue, and violet. These colors create a more formal mood and can make a small room appear larger.

Below: A blue-and-white wall quilt continues the color scheme of this blue-and-white kitchen.

ACCENT WITH A STRONG COLOR. A strong, dark color, such as red, black, or cobalt blue, provides a dramatic accent against an all-white background. Two-color quilts, usually made from white or off-white plus a strong solid color, work well with this color scheme.

DRAW ON THE PAST. If your quilts are from a certain era, try to use colors from that period in your decorating scheme. Deep, dark colors—turkey red, indigo, brown, and black—were popular background colors in late-nineteenth-century fabrics. A rainbow of bright pastels were used in the 1930s—bubble gum pink, butter yellow, robin's egg blue, and "that green."

Ever-popular 1930s colors brighten the quilts and pillows on this daybed.

USE COMPLEMENTARY COLORS. Color schemes that use two complementary colors make a strong graphic statement. Many traditional color schemes, such as red and green or purple and yellow, are based on this idea. The secret of a successful two-color decorating scheme is to use both colors in all areas of the room. Use a color wheel to help choose colors, remembering that opposite colors are complements and therefore intensify each other.

STICK TO ONE COLOR. Use a variety of light, medium, and dark values of a single color. The darkest shade will add depth to the decorating scheme. You may want to add a single splash of a contrasting color for visual interest.

LEFT: *A complementary color scheme of warm reds and mossy greens was used for this cozy family room.*

OPPOSITE: *A variety of light, medium, and dark blue tones contribute to this restful bedroom.*

Is There a Theme or Focus?

Use color or a theme to tie fabrics together. Color can link fabrics together, so be sure the same tones appear in each of the prints used. Often a theme further unifies fabrics, such as a floral motif, a sports motif, or a novelty print such as birdhouses, teapots, or sailboats. A collection of objects can set a theme for a room and help you select colors and fabrics. Gather your treasures together in one spot for decorating impact.

A quilt collection mixes nicely on shelves with pottery and dishes.

Quilts All Through the House

Quilts add warmth and comfort wherever they are used—you don't need to limit them to bedrooms. Quilts and small quilted accent pieces are perfectly at home in dining rooms, kitchens, laundry rooms, and even bathrooms. If you follow good conservation practices, these textile treasures can add to your decor without being sacrificed.

The following pages provide a tour of seven homes where quilts have been used prominently in the decor. Viewing the homes as separate units will give you a sense of the owner's decorating style and the unity among the color schemes in each room. I hope these examples inspire you and suggest possible directions for your home.

The living room of Diana and Chris Schmidt (see pages 54–59) features two Postage Stamp quilts (on the chairs) and a variety of collectibles.

An Architect's Inspiration

Twenty years ago, the Jarvis family of Woodinville, Washington, hired an architect to design a contemporary home for their secluded, wooded setting. Now, with their children grown, they decided the house neeeded an interior revamp.

Fresh, airy colors, lacy linens, hand-stitched quilts, and numerous collectibles enhance every room. Indeed, the Jarvises' personal touch is evident in the collections displayed throughout, especially the old gas lamps. Refurbished and re-wired, the lamps add a nostalgic touch to every room.

This family loves to cook and entertain on a grand scale, and their gracious home provides a spacious setting for family parties and social events. A large kitchen, open to the family room, is the heart of the home. Here, the gentleman chef of the house can create gourmet specialties at the cooking island while guests watch.

While some owners might decorate this contemporary home with modern furnishings, the Jarvises used a light touch and numerous antiques to give their home a warm Country feeling.

OPPOSITE: *The living room features a wall of glass overlooking a densely wooded area. Swagged valances, soft colors, lacy linens, and lots of quilts help soften the angular lines created by a vaulted ceiling.*

OPPOSITE: *Two wing chairs hold coordinated pillows and quilts. A miniature quilt joins dolls, samplers, paintings, and a clock to create an interesting visual composition on the wall.*

ABOVE: *In this inviting setting, a pastel quilt is set off by coordinating tapestry pillows, sofa fabric, and a hand-painted chest used as a coffee table.*

OPPOSITE: Chintz fabric, used throughout the kitchen and family room, unites the two areas.

BELOW: Lacy linens and pastel quilts contrast with the rough textures of the bricks and wood.

OPPOSITE: Quilts add a splash of color to this soft pastel color scheme.

BELOW: The antique brass bed holds a wealth of fabric treasures: plaid bolsters tied to the headboard, lace pillow shams, ruffled brocade pillowcases, and silk accent pillows.

In Tune with Nature

Joan and Bill Colvins' home, which they designed and built, opens to the spectacular Pacific Northwest scenery surrounding it. Joan, a quilt artist, is especially sensitive to the natural beauty of the water and nature around her, and often interprets these themes in her subtly colored quilts.

Natural textures abound inside the Colvin home, from the aggregate floors and walls of the front foyer to the wood floors, trim, and detail of the room interiors. The muted color scheme used in each room—black, beige, tan, taupe, and gray—complements, rather than competes with, the natural beauty outside.

Joan's studio is a compact space with bountiful storage behind louvered doors. The studio is open to the main living area and has an outdoor view. Natural light spills in from three skylights.

The rear of the house offers views of sea and mountains. The outside deck and moonwalk are wonderful spaces for relaxing in the calm of the evening.

Opposite: "Trumpeter Swans," an original quilt by Joan, makes a stunning focal point

YAMAHA

LEFT: *Joan's "Herons" quilt adorns the wall visible from her studio*

OPPOSITE: *"Fern Fronds," another of Joan's designs, covers the bed.*

BELOW: *Three skylights provide natural light in Joan's compact studio, which is located in an alcove adjoining the living room.*

A Symphony of Light

Mary and Phil Hickey remodeled a charming home in a quiet Seattle suburb. Surrounded by large trees and graced by a creek which flows through the backyard, the home reflects the talents and myriad interests of its owners. Phil's carpentry skills and Mary's eye for color and design have transformed the interior into a symphony of light and color.

Mary is a talented quiltmaker and author, who travels both nationally and internationally to present her seminars and humorous talks. Phil, an attorney, keeps the projects moving along while Mary is away.

Mary's decorative painting abounds throughout the house, from the trompe l'oeil checkerboard fireplace tile to the quilt painted on the living room wall.

Mary's interests also extend outdoors to the lovely perennial gardens and assortment of ducks and chickens found on the property.

OPPOSITE: Lovely quilts embellish the sofas in this light-filled living room.

ABOVE: A collection of miniature quilts made by Mary fills the display space in a glass-topped coffee table.

LEFT: Mary, who enjoys decorative painting and trompe l'oeil, painted a Basket quilt on the wall.

OPPOSITE: Small quilts made by Mary form a grouping over the fireplace, while other pastel quilts cover the table and sofa back.

The soft green color scheme provides a restful bedroom setting. To add punch, Mary used a green–and–white striped fabric for the window valance, chairs, and one wall.

ABOVE: The entryway on the main floor is decorated for the summer holidays and introduces visitors to Mary's interests: quiltmaking and sailing.

OPPOSITE: Mary's sewing studio, located on the lower level, allows plenty of room for storage.

An Abundance of Elegance

Felicia Holtzinger's home is situated in a colorful apple orchard. The surrounding hills, covered with orchards, can be viewed from almost every window and again from the wraparound porch. The front porch is home to Adirondack-style chairs, made from apple-box pallets by her son, Mark.

Felicia's natural talent for decorating is evident throughout the house. The decor is dramatic, upscale, and bound to be noticed. She has a natural flair for organizing and arranging, no doubt influenced by her art background.

Felicia's quilt collection began as an outgrowth of research done at the Yakima Valley Museum. Her collection of miniature quilts was featured in Sandi Fox's book *Small Endearments*. The quilts have since been donated to the Los Angeles County Museum.

Quilts blend readily with her other collectibles—majolica, porcelain, wicker, lace, and angels. The home's interior, with its calm wood tones and massive oak beams, offers many places to display Felicia's collections.

OPPOSITE: *Ralph Lauren plaid and floral fabrics accent the cushions on the wicker furniture in this large dining room. A quilt covers the table, which is laden with interesting objects. Additional colorful quilts are hung from the second-floor railing.*

LEFT: *An array of miniature objects and a floral topper over an antique quilt add interest and color to this quiet corner.*

BELOW: *Exposed ceiling beams and twig furniture create a rustic look in the living room.*

OPPOSITE: *Antique quilts brighten the second-floor hallway.*

ABOVE: An antique quilt and an abundance of interesting objects and collectibles fill this delightful nursery.

OPPOSITE: Quilts and twig beds have a natural affinity for each other, as shown in this lovely room. The bed is swathed in clouds of sheer fabric, creating a very feminine feel.

A Remodel—Start to Finish

Dan and Nancy Martin fell in love with the 180° view of this getaway on waterfront property. Originally built in 1914 and remodeled in 1978, it had dark woodwork, outdated windows, harvest gold appliances, and shag carpets.

Nancy felt the 1970s remodel wasn't true to the original character of the beach cottage and began to plan a major renovation project. Working with interior designer Anita Yesland, they altered the floor plan to take advantage of the views and enhance wall space for hanging quilts. The main living area of the house offers views of the Cascade Mountains and downtown Seattle across Puget Sound.

The Martins changed the placement and orientation of all the rooms, except the two bathrooms and a guest bedroom. They also moved the front door to the side of the house. Now the first thing you see when entering the house is a view of the water and mountains through the living room and foyer windows. A stairway takes you to the second-floor walkway.

OPPOSITE: The main living area of the house includes the kitchen, dining room, and living room, all with views of the water. Quilts are folded over the chair and sofa.

RIGHT: *Tree blocks in several variations are found in the quilts on the wall and table, as well as the patchwork pillow and twig wall shelves.*

OPPOSITE: *Raising part of the ceiling in the main living area opens up the space and allows a second-story loft to project into the room. A Log Cabin quilt hangs from the loft railing.*

OPPOSITE: *The guest bedroom is decorated with an assortment of red-and-white quilts. Coordinating fabric used in the quilt, tablecloth, pillow shams, scalloped dust ruffle, window valance, and small slipper chair gives the room a unified look.*

RIGHT: *Additional red-and-white quilts hang from a peg rack in the corner of the guest room.*

LEFT: *An upstairs bedroom boasts a nautical theme: Ocean Waves quilts on the twin beds, fish fabric on the slipcovered headboards, and Marine Corps memorabilia. An Anvil quilt (left) and Milky Way quilt (right) serve as accents.*

RIGHT: A collection of pink-and-white plates sets the theme for the master bath.

BELOW: The warm reds and greens in the guest bath were inspired by the delightful Santa quilt reflected in the mirror.

OPPOSITE: Soft beige walls, light wood floors, a window wall with an arched top, and a new vaulted ceiling combine to create a calm, tranquil feeling in the master bedroom. A custom-made cabinet serves both as dresser and headboard, allowing the bed to be placed in the center of the room, facing the view.

A Touch of Folk Art

Diana and Chris Schmidt have decorated their 1929 vintage home with folk art, quilts, and a marvelous collection of antiques.

Diana, an artist in her own right, has skillfully combined the exuberant colors of Southwest pottery and wood carvings with her quilts. Most of the Mexican folk art you see was purchased on trips to galleries in Tucson and Santa Barbara.

This grand home features magnificent detailing and handcrafted touches. Originally built by a sheep rancher, the house sits high on a hill and affords breathtaking views of nearby snow-capped mountain peaks. The house wraps around an outdoor courtyard, complete with fireplace, providing the perfect spot for summer entertaining.

Tile floors, beveled-glass windows, beamed ceilings, and arched doorways add interesting architectural touches throughout the home.

Colorful Oriental rugs and woven carpets soften the tile floors.

Diana's knack for creating vignettes and displays is evident throughout the house; one hardly knows where to look first. The added color and texture provided by quilts make this a most inviting home.

OPPOSITE: *An overview of the living room showcases many of Diana's collections. The table in the foreground displays Southwest pottery figures and a wonderful antique rocking horse. See page 19 for another view of the living room.*

LEFT: *Antique Staffordshire china is arranged on a glass tabletop that protects a Rose of Sharon quilt.*

BELOW: *Wide window ledges in the hallway provide wonderful display space for quilts and collectibles.*

An appliqué quilt brightens the hallway. Additional quilts are folded on the shelf above the door.

ABOVE: *This relaxing guest room features an antique scrap quilt spread across the brass bed. Flannel pillow shams in buffalo checks and plaid add colorful accents.*

OPPOSITE: *An Amish quilt covers an antique canopy bed in the master bedroom. Classic quilts hang over the quilt rack at the foot of the bed.*

Seasonal Changes

The home of Dan and Nancy Martin features a display of quilts that changes seasonally. Shown here in its Christmas finery, the red, green, and blue color scheme sparkles against a crisp white background.

The Martin home is located in a small neighborhood known as "The Homestead." Eighteen different Colonial homes and a common green area nestle on a wooded cul-de-sac. Wide-plank wood floors, Colonial moldings and beams, bull's-eye glass, and small-paned windows all combine to create a warm backdrop for the Martins' quilt collection.

Dan appreciates the outdoor environment surrounding their home, which is located on Cottage Lake Creek, a salmon-spawning stream. A fish ladder in the backyard allows the Martins to view sev-

eral species of salmon swimming upstream to spawn.

Nancy, a quiltmaker, author, and quilting teacher, travels internationally to teach and lecture. Nancy and Dan are owners of That Patchwork Place, Inc.

OPPOSITE: *The "keeping room" is an open area that combines living room, dining room, and kitchen. Wide-plank pine floors and a soft color scheme unify these three areas. Christmas quilts and pillows add holiday cheer.*

LEFT: *Fabric Santas surround the fireplace, and a collection of Eldreth pottery Santas decorates the mantle.*

BELOW: *Window coverings and pillows coordinate the holiday color scheme.*

ABOVE: *A handmade Santa on the coffee table rings in the season.*

RIGHT: *A festive striped floral fabric covers the window seat, pillows, and ruffled chair cushions.*

The warm red walls of the den complement the Feathered Star quilt hanging above the sofa.

SUGGESTED READING

Selected Books from
THAT PATCHWORK PLACE

Borders by Design • *Paulette Peters*
The Easy Art of Appliqué • *Mimi Dietrich &
    Roxi Eppler*
Easy Machine Paper Piecing • *Carol Doak*
Happy Endings • *Mimi Dietrich*
The Joy of Quilting • *Joan Hanson & Mary Hickey*
Little Quilts • *Alice Berg, Sylvia Johnson &
    Mary Ellen Von Holt*
Loving Stitches • *Jeana Kimball*
Machine Quilting Made Easy • *Maurine Noble*
Patchwork Basics • *Marie-Christine Flocard &
    Cosabeth Parriaud*
A Perfect Match • *Donna Lynn Thomas*
Quick & Easy Quiltmaking • *Mary Hickey,
    Nancy J. Martin, Marsha McCloskey &
    Sara Nephew*
The Quilters' Companion
    • *Compiled by That Patchwork Place*
Quilts for Baby • *Ursula Reikes*
Rotary Riot • *Judy Hopkins & Nancy J. Martin*
ScrapMania • *Sally Schneider*
Sensational Settings • *Joan Hanson*
Shortcuts: A Concise Guide to Rotary Cutting
    • *Donna Lynn Thomas*
Simply Scrappy Quilts • *Nancy J. Martin*
Treasures from Yesteryear, Books One & Two
    • *Sharon Newman*
Watercolor Quilts • *Pat Magaret & Donna Slusser*

These quilting books are available at quilt, craft, and bookstores. Call 1-800-426-3126 for the name of the quilt shop nearest you.

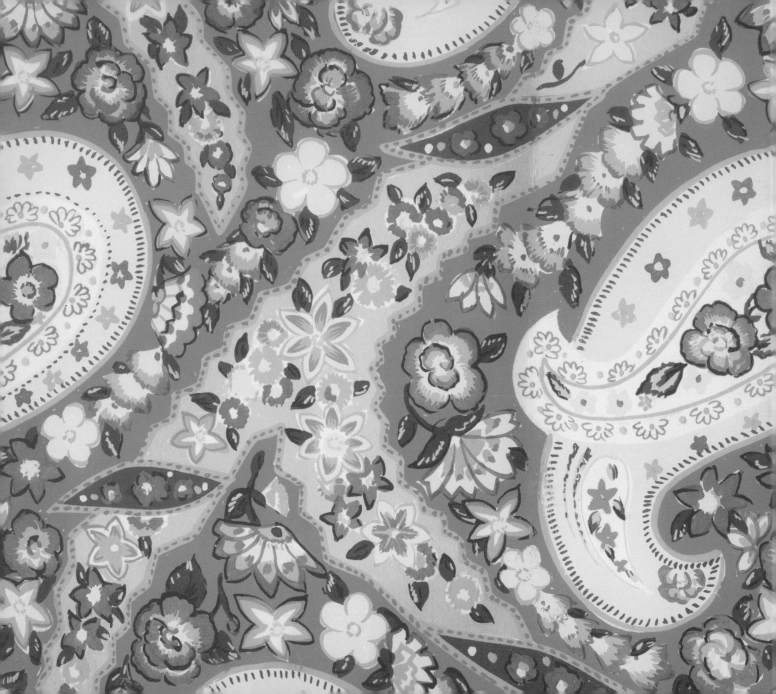